W9-BXZ-192

CARVE

CARVE

A SIMPLE GUIDE TO WHITTLING

MELANIE ABRANTES

CLARKSON POTTER/PUBLISHERS

NEW YORK

TO MY MOM AND DAD:

thank you for working hard and
teaching me to do the same

Published in the United States by Clarkson
Potter/Publishers, an imprint of the Crown
Publishing Group, a division of Penguin
Random House LLC, New York.
crownpublishing.com
clarksonpotter.com

CLARKSON POTTER is a trademark and
POTTER with colophon is a registered trademark
of Penguin Random House LLC.

Library of Congress Cataloging-in-Publication
Data
Names: Abrantes, Melanie, author.
Title: Carve: a simple guide to whittling /
Melanie Abrantes;
photographs by Melanie Riccardi.
Description: New York : Clarkson Potter, 2017.
Identifiers: LCCN 2016044123 (print) | LCCN
2016047004 (ebook) | ISBN 9780451498960

(hardback) | ISBN 9780451498977 (ebook)
Subjects: LCSH: Wood-carving—Patterns. |
Wood-carving—Technique. | BISAC: CRAFTS &
HOBBIES / Woodwork. | CRAFTS & HOBBIES /
Carving. | HOUSE & HOME / Woodworking.
Classification: LCC TT199.7 .A27 2017 (print) |
LCC TT199.7 (ebook) | DDC 736/.4—dc23
LC record available at https://lccn.loc.
gov/2016044123

ISBN 978-0-451-49896-0
Ebook ISBN 978-0-451-49897-7

Printed in China

Cover and book design by Stephanie Huntwork
Cover and interior photographs by
Melanie Riccardi
Prop styling by Genevieve Bandrowski

10 9 8 7 6 5 4 3 2 1

First Edition

CONTENTS

72

96

52

63

102

42

84

INTRODUCTION

A WOODEN SPATULA FOR STIRRING A FAVORITE STEW, a simple tray for holding keys, an elegant comb for brushing your hair . . . the possibilities of things you can make with a knife and a piece of wood are endless.

Whittling is an art that has been honed on porches for hundreds of years by both experts and laypeople who take pleasure in the simple act of molding a scrap of wood into something unique. As a professional woodworker, I've taken to this old-fashioned pastime because I can do it anytime, anywhere—not just in my wood shop, but at a barbecue with friends or on a camping trip. And as a designer, I tend to give whittled objects my own modern spin, creating iconic items that are not only useful around the house but also beautiful enough to give as a gift.

You might think creating such polished objects would be easy for me because of my day job, but you, too, can master the art of whittling. Even if you've never held a knife before, a few easy techniques are all you need to learn. It helps if the object you're carving is small in size and straightforward in shape (good to know that some of the most stylish objects have the simplest lines!). And while you can stick with your trusty knife, by adding a few more simple tools—like a gouge for scooping concave shapes and some sandpaper for buffing out dints—you can carve better items faster. Whether you have one tool or three, this book will walk you through everything you need to know to make, personalize, and maintain your treasured piece.

There's something meditative and therapeutic about pushing a knife into grain. It's a hobby that pulls you into the present moment and helps you focus on the task at hand. It can be a sustainable way to add accessories to your kitchen or living room, and how cool is it that something you've spent just a few hours making will last for decades with a little care: I hope these projects provide hours of inspiration and entertainment. Now it's time to pick up your knife, choose a piece of wood, and carve!

GETTING STARTED

LEARNING HOW TO CARVE IS LESS ABOUT FOLLOWING a specific set of instructions than it is about gaining an understanding of how your hands work with your knife—and that synergy just comes with practice. I think you'll find that whittling skills are rather easy to master; after you finish a few projects, you'll start to feel more comfortable with your tools and want to take on more intricate designs.

THE WHITTLER'S TOOLBOX

Purists will say that a knife is the only tool you need to whittle—your trusted pocketknife will do just fine as long as it's sharp, but you may find that a proper carving knife is more efficient and exact. Using the right blade as well as a few more tools will help you make better projects faster. When you're shopping for new tools, keep the following tips in mind.

THE KNIFE

The only carving tool you will need for most of these projects is a knife (though a gouge comes in handy to hollow out wood, such as for the bowl of a spoon). I prefer the traditional Japanese *kiridashi kogatana,* a versatile knife great for just about anything—from pencil sharpening to intricate carving.

TIPS FOR BUYING NEW TOOLS

- **Focus on fit and comfort.** If you have small hands, start with a small knife. You'll feel more confident cutting with a tool you can control. Don't forget to take your handedness into account when buying a knife that's beveled (or angled) on one side.

- **Choose good-quality steel.** Hard steel laminated with soft steel will hold a sharp edge longer. Buy from a manufacturer with a solid reputation: the Japanese company that supplies my knives has been in business for 250 years.

- **Heed the cutting edge.** A knife that is beveled on one side will carve a sharper edge than a double-beveled blade because the surface is thinner.

- **Buy the right-size blade.** A long edge is ideal for a large, complex project that requires you to remove a lot of wood. A short edge is a good fit for beginners and travelers; it is also better for carving intricate designs.

- **Invest in something you love.** If you do, it will serve you well in the long run. Take it from someone who started out with cheap tools. When my first knife broke, I spent more money to buy a better replacement—and the quality of my work improved dramatically.

THE GOUGE

A gouge is a tool that scoops into the wood to create shallow hollows and surface designs. It is defined by both the curve of its edge, referred to as its sweep, and the shape of its end—one that is 12 millimeters will give you the most versatility. I prefer to use a Japanese-style spoon gouge that looks like a printmaking linocut tool, except for the slight upward curve at the end, which helps me to shovel out wood. For me, the easy push of a gouge is more intuitive than the scooping action of a Western-style whittling hook, and it is flexible for making patterns (see page 113). A gouge also holds a sharp edge, so I can save time when finishing a project.

ADDING TO YOUR TOOLBOX

The following tools are by no means necessary for whittling, but as you get more involved in your new hobby, you may want to supplement your trusted knife. They will help you to shape and refine more intricate objects, or pare down larger pieces of wood to make smaller items.

1. **Gouge** for carving shallow concave shapes; sizes vary (see page 15)
2. **Right-angle ruler** for drawing templates with straight lines and angles
3. **Rasp or file** for filing down tough ends and edges
4. **Hand planer** for shaving wood down to size or filing straight edges
5. **Mallet** for hammering a gouge or a chisel to create deeper cuts
6. **Saw** for cutting smaller pieces of wood from large chunks (see page 31)
7. **Carving gloves or leather thumb guard** for preventing cuts and calluses
8. **Beeswax** for sealing your piece (see page 116)
9. **Compass** for making perfect circles
10. **Sandpaper** for finishing your piece
11. **Duster** for cleaning your piece
12. **Whetstone** for sharpening your knife (see page 20)

1.

2.

3.

4.

5.

6.

7.

8.

9.

10.

11.

12.

PLAY IT SAFE

Before we begin, here are a few tips for dealing with sharp objects.

- Keep your tools sharp; dull tools can be more dangerous (see page 20).

- Always be conscious about where your hand is in relation to the tool. It's easy to slip and cut yourself when you're not paying attention.

- People most often get hurt when they're putting their knife away or playing around, so never let your guard down, even when you're not working.

- Sit in a comfortable space so your arms have plenty of room to move. Establish your "blood circle": Boy Scouts create a safety circle of at least an arm's length away from other people before they begin whittling.

- Don't whittle on the go, and be conscious about carving in public spaces where knives may be prohibited.

- Wear a leather thumb guard or carving gloves to protect your hands from calluses and minor cuts. Donning gloves will make it easier for you to work in tight crevices.

- Always have a first-aid kit on hand. Clean and bandage a minor cut. Go straight to the emergency room for treatment of a major wound.

- Children should always be supervised when using tools.

HOW TO SHARPEN YOUR KNIFE

You're more likely to hurt yourself with blunt tools, so be sure to sharpen your knife from time to time as you whittle. Advanced carvers sharpen their knives every few hours as they work on a project. How will you know if your knife is sharp enough? Test its performance by trying to cut through several sheets of paper or a magazine. If the knife easily cuts through the paper, then you're ready to work. If it catches in any spot, sharpen it before you start your project. That way you won't have to press too hard on the wood or saw through it.

Bowl or other container (big enough to fit the whetstone)

1,000-grit whetstone

Hand towel (optional)

Several sheets of printer paper

Whittling knife

Colored permanent marker (I prefer a bright color as black is not as easy to see against the steel shavings)

1. Fill the bowl with water and submerge the whetstone for 10 minutes and then place it on a flat surface. It should still be a little wet. (To keep the stone from moving around, you can set it on a hand towel spread out on the surface.)

2. Fold the top left corner of a sheet of paper to the right side to make a 45° angle (as if you were making a paper airplane). Fold the paper in half again to make a 22.5° angle and in half again to make an 11.25° angle. The angle at which you'll want to hold the knife will lie somewhere between these last two folds, depending on the bevel of the knife. As you hold the knife on the stone, you can use this folded paper to check your angles.

DON'T BE DULL

You can skip this exercise altogether by bringing your tools to a kitchen store that specializes in knife sharpening, but I think it's important for you to learn how to do this yourself. Mastering this technique is another way to get to know your knife and develop the steady hand skills that you'll need for carving.

3. Determine the angle of the knife's bevel. The manufacturer may be able to supply this information, or you can measure it yourself: Lay the bevel down on the stone and use the folded paper to measure the angle between the stone and the flat edge, or cheek, of the knife.

4. Lay your knife on the whetstone bevel side up. Use the permanent marker to ink the entire beveled edge of the knife's blade. As you sharpen the knife, the ink will disappear from the blade, allowing you to check for sharpness.

5. Hold the knife with your dominant hand and press your thumb down on the blade to steady it. Place your other hand on the stone for leverage. Pull the knife along the length of the stone at the appropriate angle 5 to 10 times, depending on how dull it is. If the knife is double-beveled, flip it and repeat. Continue sharpening the knife until the ink disappears.

6. The blade is properly sharpened when it can easily cut through paper.

TO THE POINT

If you're working with a vintage knife that won't get sharp, you will need to decrease the angle of the bevel. This requires distinctive tools, so I recommend going to a hardware or kitchen store that specializes in knife sharpening.

WHITTLING TECHNIQUES

Whittling relies on a few easy cuts. If you're a beginner, don't stress about creating a polished piece. Rather, focus on sharpening your skills.

THE PUSH CUT

Use the push cut to skim the wood, especially when you're close to the final shape. Hold the wood securely in your nondominant hand. Position the blade on the wood at a slight angle (going with the grain, so that the shavings curl). Place your nondominant thumb on the back (dull side) of the blade, pushing the knife into the wood to remove small, shallow shavings. For more precision and more power, you can place your dominant thumb on the other thumb to help push the knife.

TIP: Never force the knife through the wood; if it slips, you risk cutting yourself. You can feel when the knife is going against the grain (or if the wood pushes back). If the knife sticks, flip your piece around and try cutting the opposite way.

THE PULL OR PARING CUT

Use the pull or paring cut to get into tight spaces or to create perpendicular lines (such as where the handle of a spatula will meet the base of the flat blade). Grasp the knife in your dominant hand (as you would the handle of a motorcycle) and hold the wood securely in your nondominant hand. Place your dominant thumb on the wood and the blade at a slight angle on the wood. Squeeze the knife toward you using your thumb as leverage (as if you were peeling an apple).

THE POWER CUT

Use the power cut to remove big chunks of wood. Hold the wood securely in your nondominant hand, grasp the knife in your dominant hand, and cut with the grain and away from you using long strokes, being careful not to lose control of the knife. Angling your blade deep into the wood will increase the amount you remove, but be mindful as you carve; if the wood's grain is naturally too loose, you may inadvertently start to cut off a large chunk. If that happens, don't panic: just flip the piece and cut in the opposite direction to save that chunk.

TIP: Test these skills by making the river stones (page 72), one of the easiest projects in the book.

THE STOP CUT

Use the stop cut to create perpendicular angles or
carve notches in the wood for removing material. Hold
the wood securely in your nondominant hand, grasp
the knife in your dominant hand, and push the blade
of the knife with your thumb against the grain and into
the wood to make a simple notch. You can rock your
knife back and forth to deepen or lengthen the notch
into a line. To remove a small triangular piece of wood,
use a push cut to carve into the notch; the knife will stop
at the notch. Continue stop cutting and push cutting to
achieve your desired depth.

THE V CUT

The V cut is similar to the stop cut and is great for adding detailing like engraving to personalize a piece. Hold
the wood securely in your nondominant hand and grasp
the knife in your dominant hand. Push the blade of the
knife with your thumb against the grain and at an angle
into the wood to make a simple notch. Turn your knife
blade to the opposite angle and pull or pare cut back the
other way to create a V in the wood. Continue V cutting
to achieve your desired depth.

CHOOSING THE RIGHT WOOD

Strolling through a forest, picking up a stick, and starting to whittle is a pleasant notion (and you can certainly do this!), but there are practical pros and cons of working with wet versus dry wood.

Live or wet wood is what you find in your backyard or in the forest.

Pros: No planning is needed to whittle live wood; you can start your project on a whim or while camping. It's also great for beginners because it's softer to cut and faster to finish. There is a special pride in whittling a piece of locally sourced wood, log to finish. If you're going for a whimsical appearance, your piece will look more organic than if you used dry kiln.

Cons: Large logs need to be split, stripped, and cut down to the right proportions. And because the water hasn't evaporated in the wood, your finished piece will require additional handling to prevent it from warping or twisting (which happens once the water evaporates).

Dry kiln wood has been processed and is ready for purchase.

Pros: Dry wood is more stable than live or wet wood: it won't warp or move and will generally keep its shape once you carve it. Many varieties are available year-round. Check out the selection of scraps to sort through at your local lumberyard. A minimum purchase may be required, but you might score some free scraps if you ask nicely.

Cons: If the lumberyard doesn't stock small scraps, you'll need to saw the wood down to size. Some types of dry wood, like walnut, are much harder to cut than others, like pine, which can be frustrating for beginners.

DRYING OUT LIVE WOOD

There are certain steps you can take to dry out a piece of live wood, but there's always a chance it will warp. First, carve the live wood down to the appropriate size for whittling (but don't whittle it just yet). Place the wood and wood shavings (which will absorb any moisture) in a paper bag and store in a dark, dry place for at least two weeks, depending on the size. Check the bag: Does the wood feel dry to the touch? Has it lost its timber smell? Once it's thoroughly dry, whittle it and then let it rest in a dry, sunny place before you stain, wax, or seal the piece.

While you may fall in love with the color and grain of a particular variety of wood, you'll want to choose one that's appropriate for both the use of the piece and your skill level as a carver. The darker the wood, the harder it will be to carve; however, hardwoods have a nicer finish and tend to last longer than softwoods. Fantastic options for beginners are the really soft and inexpensive pine, poplar, and bass.

CUTTING WOOD TO SIZE

Start with a block of wood that's as close in size as possible to your template, to save yourself from push cutting all afternoon with few results. You can find precut pieces at craft stores, but your selection will be limited to the types they stock (big-box stores seem to carry only bass and pine). Specialty stores like Woodcraft stock bundles of small cuts and different wood varieties, and your local hardware store can cut lumber into more manageable blocks for you. It's a good idea to have access to a simple handsaw and clamp to make quick work of petite projects like spoons, or ask a friendly neighbor who has a band saw to help you out. Before buying a handsaw, ask to test it out to find one that fits your hand.

To use a handsaw, secure the wood to a work surface with an F-style clamp. The portion you are cutting should be hanging off the edge so that your handsaw doesn't hit the surface. Be aware of which way the teeth are facing (my Japanese saw cuts when I pull rather than push it). Before starting to work, put on safety glasses and gloves. Saw the wood down to your desired size. I like to cut out a few pieces at a time, so that I don't have to keep dragging out my saw.

GO WITH THE GRAIN

My favorite wood varieties,
from left to right:

BASS

CHERRY

MAHOGANY

BUCKEYE BURL

WALNUT

DESIGNING YOUR PIECE

If this is your first time whittling, use the templates (see pages 118–123) and instructions for making any of the objects in this book. Once you've completed a project, you'll probably start thinking about how you can make it different the next time: carving a longer handle for a spatula to reach into your deepest pot, for instance. Soon every object you look at will inspire you; these tips will help you turn that inspiration into action.

• Designate a sketch pad or a notebook as your whittling journal. Choose one with graph paper if you're concerned about consistency.

• Research and collect your inspirations so you can understand what you like and why.

• Using inspiration that you've collected, put your ideas on paper by sketching your object.

• Draw your object as a template proportionally (here's where graph paper comes in handy), using very simple lines.

• Cut out and trace your template onto a piece of wood. You'll sand out any marks on the wood.

• Use the techniques on pages 23 to 31.

CARVING
THE BOOK

River stone, page 72

EAT

CHOPSTICKS

EASY

IN MANY WESTERN HOUSEHOLDS, THESE EASTERN utensils might make an appearance at the table only for takeout, but they're a staple in my kitchen. I use them to devour my favorite rice bowls, and I tend to grab a pair instead of tongs while cooking, so having a sturdy set on hand is important. Luckily, their beautiful, simple form is easy and fun to master with a whittling knife. The most difficult part is making sure they end up symmetrical, but a little variation just sets them apart from mass-produced versions. Rest these on a river stone (see page 72) to keep them from rolling off your table.

Carving gloves or leather thumb guard

Whittling knife

2 pieces of walnut, cherry, or cypress wood,
cut lengthwise with the grain to 7 x ¼ x ¼ inches

100-, 150-, and 220-grit sandpapers, cut to 2 x 3 inches

Soft 100% cotton cloth

Food-grade mineral oil

(continued)

1. Use the whittling knife to pare one piece of wood down to a long cylinder; take long, thin push-cut strokes (see page 23) with the grain from the middle of the wood to the end. Rotate the wood as you cut to achieve an even shape; because the piece is thin, be careful not to remove large chunks all at once. Repeat with the second piece of wood.

2. Taper one chopstick to about ⅜ inch in diameter at one end and 1 centimeter at the other end (use the template on page 120, or you can measure it with a ruler). Repeat with the second chopstick.

3. Sand the chopsticks with the grain until the wood is smooth and no knife marks remain. Begin sanding with the 100 grit and work your way up to the 220 grit as each sandpaper dulls.

4. Use the cotton cloth to rub the chopsticks with a layer of mineral oil and let dry for at least 30 minutes. Reapply the oil as needed, after washing the chopsticks by hand, especially if you use them as much as I use mine.

TIP: Once you get more comfortable with whittling techniques, you can personalize these chopsticks by adding details like notches, spirals, or a ball to the top of the handle before you sand it. Or embellish the ends by dipping them in paint (just not the ends you use to eat).

WINE STOPPER

EASY

THIS STOPPER MAY BE THE ONE THING THAT KEEPS ME from drinking a whole bottle of rosé in one sitting! If you've ever wondered what to do with leftover wine corks, here's your answer: turn them into permanent bottle stoppers, quick-to-make gifts for those last-minute holiday parties. As a product designer, I'm aware of the need for modern, simple barware. You can use this uncomplicated design as a jumping-off point to create shapes that suit your style. Carve a cylinder, monogram it, color-block it . . . the only limit is your own imagination.

Pencil

1 piece of buckeye burl or maple wood, cut lengthwise with the grain to 1 x 1 x 2½ inches

1 wine cork, the top trimmed by 1 inch

Carving gloves or leather thumb guard

Whittling knife

100-, 150-, and 220-grit sandpapers, cut to 2 x 3 inches

Stain or paint (optional)

Wood glue

Painter's tape

(continued)

1. Using the template on page 119, draw the shape of the stopper on both sides of the wood. Then, using the cork top as a template, draw a circle on the end of the piece that matches the diameter of the cork top (about ¾ inch).

2. Put on the carving gloves. Using the whittling knife, push-cut (see page 23) to begin rounding out the corners of the wood to create a lightbulb shape—fatter at the top and tapered at the bottom.

3. Using the push cut, taper the bottom of your piece so that it matches the diameter of the cork top. Round the top of the stopper into the shape of a dome, push cutting in a spiral direction until all of the ends are gone. Be mindful of symmetry.

4. Sand the stopper with the grain until the wood is even and smooth. Sand the bottom of the stopper until it is flat. Begin sanding with the 100 grit and work your way up to the 220 grit as each sandpaper dulls. Stain or paint your stopper (see page 114).

5. Apply the wood glue to the flat part of the stopper and attach to the top of the cork. Bind the two pieces together tightly with the painter's tape. Let the glue dry for about 12 hours before removing the tape.

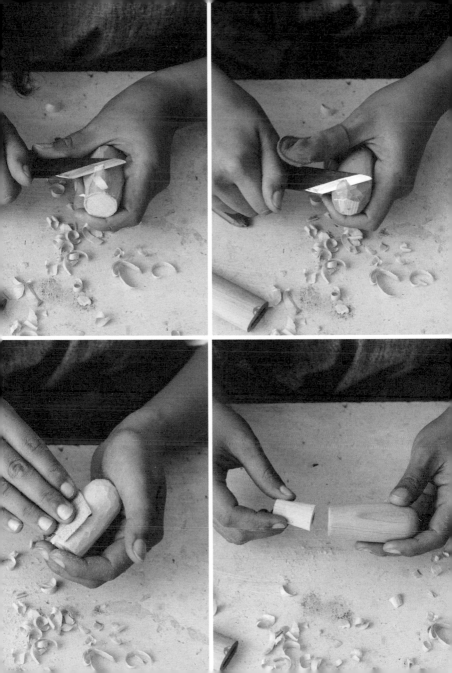

COFFEE SPOON

HARD

WHAT BETTER WAY TO HONOR YOUR MORNING POUR-
over than with a handcrafted coffee scoop? The wooden
spoon may be the most iconic whittling project—whole
books have been written about them, and hundreds
have been tagged on Instagram. This utensil is specially
meant for spooning dry beans into your coffeemaker
or cone (no washing necessary!); to use it for stirring,
you'll need to treat it with mineral oil and beeswax (see
page 116). Don't even bother putting this spoon away—
leave it out on your counter for all to admire.

Pencil

**1 piece of walnut, cherry, or mahogany wood,
cut lengthwise with the grain to 5½ x 2 x 2 inches**

Carving gloves or leather thumb guard

Whittling knife and gouge

100-, 150-, and 220-grit sandpaper, cut to 2 x 3 inches

Your choice of stain (see page 114)

Soft 100% cotton cloth

Food-grade mineral oil or beeswax

(continued)

1. Using the template on page 122, outline the top and side of the spoon on the wood. Put on the carving gloves. Using the whittling knife, push-cut (see page 23) to carve the wood down to the shape. Draw a circle about $\frac{1}{8}$ inch from the edge of your spoon to serve as a guideline for the bowl.

2. Hold the gouge in your dominant hand. To carve the bowl of the spoon, push the gouge away from you while you hold down the handle with your other hand. You can also position the wood on the bench hook (see page 71) for more support. Start in the middle of the bowl and work outward toward the circle you drew, rotating the wood and making small cuts until you reach the guideline. Once you've removed the first layer of wood, work back to the middle of the bowl, rotating it until you have carved all the way around (A).

3. Keep carving until you reach your desired depth; use your thumb and forefinger to measure the thickness of the bowl. Keep the sides and bottom of the bowl as even as possible: if you dig too deep a hole, a weak spot will form.

4. Turn the spoon over and draw a small circle in the middle of the back of the bowl to mark the thinnest

(continued)

part. Whittle the back of the spoon using a combination of push cuts and pull cuts (see page 24), carving with the grain as much as possible to create a curved back; avoid the small circled section so you don't cut through the bowl **(B)**.

5. Cut off and smooth the long sides of the handle; to get the most even results, rotate the spoon the same way you did when carving the bowl **(C)**. Use the push cut to taper the spoon at the neck to a thickness of about ¼ inch.

6. Whittle the end of the handle to round it out using push cuts (as you did for the back of the bowl), but keep it wide: the spoon should taper like a cone from the handle to the neck.

7. Sand the spoon with the grain until the wood is even and smooth **(D)**. Begin sanding with the 100 grit and work your way up to the 220 grit as each sandpaper dulls.

8. Stain the spoon as desired (see page 114). If you are going to use the spoon for stirring, use the cotton cloth to rub it with a layer of mineral oil and let dry for at least 30 minutes.

SPATULA

INTERMEDIATE

I DESIGNED THIS SPATULA WITH A SLANTED HEAD AND a beveled edge for more precision and versatility. The flat end is perfect for stirring soups or stews and deglazing pans for braises. Feel free to adapt the template by lengthening the handle or widening the blade to fit your biggest pots. While plastic spatulas often warp from heat, this workhorse should last for years with proper care. A few tips: don't soak it in water for very long, never put it in the dishwasher, and treat it with mineral oil every couple of months to prevent the wood from drying out and becoming brittle.

Pencil

1 piece of mahogany wood (see Tip on page 56), cut lengthwise with the grain to 2½ x 12 x ½ inches

Carving gloves or leather thumb guard

Whittling knife

100-, 150-, and 220-grit sandpapers, cut to 2 x 3 inches

Soft 100% cotton cloths

Food-grade mineral oil

Beeswax mixture (see page 116)

(continued)

1. Using the template on page 118, draw the handle and head of the spatula onto the wood. Whittle the wood with the knife to roughly the drawn shape by using power cuts (see page 25) and push cuts (see page 23). (A quicker option is to use a handsaw to shape the wood.)

2. Use push cuts to refine and round out the handle of the spatula into the dowel shape (A). Whittle the end of the handle to round it out using push cuts (B, C), tapering the tip to be 1/4 inch wide (D).

3. Use push cuts and pull cuts (see page 24) where necessary to refine the neck of the spatula, creating a slight curve in the wood where the head meets the handle (E). To better refine the neck, you may want to use the stop cut (page 26) to help you carve into the tight space.

4. Slice off the long edges of the head (F) to create a double-beveled head that is thickest at the base and thinner toward the edge, so that the edge comes to a V and creates the bevel (G).

(continued)

5. Slightly round out the four corners of the head using push cuts (**H**).

6. Sand the spatula with the grain until the wood is even and smooth. Begin sanding with the 100 grit and work your way up to the 220 grit as each sandpaper dulls. Make sure to sand the neck of the spatula well, so that you have a smooth transition from the handle to the head.

7. Use a cotton cloth to rub the spatula with a layer of mineral oil, and then use another cloth to add a layer of beeswax for extra protection. Let the spatula dry overnight before using.

TIP: Don't use exotic woods like rosewood that may leach harmful oils into your food or reclaimed lumber that may have been chemically treated or exposed to toxins. Instead, choose mahogany or another hardwood that is naturally food safe.

LIVE

66   THE TEN PRINCES

his eyes blossomed with joy as he cried: "Ah! My
dear, my very dear Apaharavarman!" Then, as his
friend sat behind he caught two sturdy arms thrust
beneath his own armpits, thus seeming to embrace
himself after which, he reached behind him and
clasped his friend. But Apaharavarman behind him
picked nuts of diverse enemy service branches, proud
of their pluck, who surged about, using bow, double-
lance, barb dart, spear, club, mace, and other assorted
weapons. A moment later he saw that army sur-
rounded by another host that doubled in front.

Presently a gentleman—blond as a wine-
am, with hair like a black gem, with hands
as fine as lilies with long eyes with hair...
ky white, with a jeweled dagger at his hip,
robe, slender and broad in waist and chest,
dexterous shafts on the hostile feet, while
soaring with his toes the rung of the ears of his fleet
approaching elephant. This man inferring from pre-
vious description that Prince Rajavahana was before
him, bowed ceremoniously, then fixed his glance on
Apaharavarman and reported: "Following your instructions as to route, this faithful group of kings has
come to the relief of the Anga sovereign. The enemy
is crushed and dispersed. Women and children
take their weapons. What next?"
Majesty," cried the delighted Apaharavar.

man, "pray grant this faithful servant the
glance. You are to consider his get-up o th
his name Dhanamitra an incognito. I y
objection, let him for the Anga king f
ment and assemble the dissipated trea
self, while Your Majesty seeks a retired
vering-place. Then let him wait upon y
der kings friendly to us "As you will,
prince, and following the indicated l
city he dismounted from the elephant
mendous banyan tree in silky and c
of wind from Ganges" billowy. Apaha
's back and seated himself already dismounted, quickly
hand a space of Ganges say
Prince sat thus, Dhanam
his obeisance, and with
nan, Archapala, Pr
s, Kamapala, lord
whole company of the
sion." And when they fir
mony. He embraced the
of Benares, Vid
He also looked with
friends and durit
embraced him

CATCHALL TRAY

HARD

EVERY CONSOLE OR NIGHTSTAND NEEDS A LITTLE
protection from your watch or the contents of your
pockets, and this little landing pad is minimalist
enough for any style. Because this project requires
more carving than others in this book, set aside five or
six hours for dedicated whittling (translation: start it
at least a week before Father's Day!). I used the gouge to
create a handsome texture for the interior of the tray;
it's a subtle detail that defines understated elegance.
Of course, you can put your own spin on this design by
choosing a different texture (see page 113 for more ideas).

Pencil

1 piece of cedar or cherry wood, cut lengthwise with the
grain to 8 x 3½ x 1 inches

Carving gloves or leather thumb guard (optional but
encouraged)

Whittling knife

Bench hook (see page 71)

Gouge

100-, 150-, and 200-grit sandpaper, cut to 2 x 3 inches

(continued)

1. Using the template on page 120, draw the outline on the wood. Using the whittling knife, push-cut (see page 23) to carve the wood to the shape.

2. Position the wood on the bench hook and use the gouge to begin whittling away the middle part of the tray, stopping just short of the handles, until the middle is ¼ inch thick **(A)**.

3. Once you have achieved a thickness of ¼ inch, create a texture by pushing the gouge down the length of the tray to carve 1-inch shallow cuts.

4. Using the whittling knife, push-cut to slice off the top edges of both handles so they are beveled **(B)**. For easy lifting, flip the tray and carve the back of the handles until they are ¼ inch thick **(C)**.

5. Slice into the neck of the handles using pull cuts (see page 24) to create a curved shape for a more stylized look.

6. Sand the handles and the outside of the tray with the grain until the wood is even and smooth, and no knife marks remain **(D)**. Begin sanding with the 100 grit and work your way up to the 220 grit as each sandpaper dulls. Sand the middle of the tray with the 220 grit just to take down the roughness—be careful not to buff out the pattern.

AIR PLANT HOLDER

INTERMEDIATE

EVERY HOME NEEDS A LITTLE GREENERY, BUT IF YOU don't want to deal with dirt, try growing an air plant or two, which are very hands-off. All they want is a monthly soak in water for about 30 minutes; after that they can hang out in this shallow boat, which is skinny enough to fit on any windowsill. No greenery, no problem: extend the length of the boat to 9 or 10 inches and you've got a simple pencil holder for your desk.

Pencil

1 piece of maple or cherry wood, cut lengthwise
with the grain to 5¼ x 1½ x 1 inches

Bench hook (see page 71) or F-style clamp

Carving gloves or leather thumb guard

Gouge

Whittling knife

100-, 150-, and 220-grit sandpapers, cut to 2 x 3 inches

Soft 100% cotton cloth

Mineral oil and water-resistant polyurethane coating
(optional)

(continued)

1. Using the template on page 118, draw the shape on the wood. Using the whittling knife, push-cut (see page 23) to carve the wood to the shape. Draw an ⅛-inch border (A).

2. Position the wood on the bench hook with a short side facing you. To carve the sides of the plant holder's bowl, push the gouge away from you, starting from each end of the guideline and working toward the middle. Always keep your nondominant hand behind the gouge, so you don't accidentally slip and cut yourself. Remove wood until the walls are about ¼ inch thick and then cut out the middle of the bowl.

3. Turn the plant holder over. Using the whittling knife, begin cutting and curving the back using push cuts (C) to slice off the corners, edges, and ends. The total thickness of the plant holder should be ¼ inch.

4. Sand the wood with the grain until it is even and smooth. Begin sanding with the 100 grit and work your way up to the 220 grit as each sandpaper dulls.

5. Use the cotton cloth to rub the plant holder with a layer of mineral oil. To make your plant holder more durable, apply a water-resistant polyurethane coating (see page 115).

MAKE YOUR OWN BENCH HOOK

A bench hook, also known as a bracing table, will help you stabilize a piece of wood while you carve; it's especially useful when you need to push a gouge across the wood's surface to make designs like ridges and rivers. You can buy an inexpensive version on Amazon (or you can use an F-style clamp), but since you need to source wood for your projects anyway, why not make your own bench hook?

Handsaw
1 piece of pine that measures at least 8 x 13 x 1 inches
Wood glue
Soft 100% cotton cloth

1. Cut the pine to the following dimensions: one 8 x 10-inch piece (A) and two 8 x 1½-inch pieces (B and C).

2. Lay piece A on a work surface with a short side facing you. Use wood glue to attach the long side of piece B to the end of piece A to make an L shape.

3. Use wood glue to attach the long side of piece C to the other end of piece A to make what resembles a stair step.

4. Clamp each end together with two F-style clamps until the glue oozes out. Use a wet cloth to wipe away excess glue. Set the bench hook aside to dry for 12 hours until secure. Remove the clamps before using.

RIVER STONES

EASY

IF YOU'RE NEW TO WHITTLING, FORGET THE STRAIGHT lines and sharp edges; start instead with this new take on the Pet Rock. These gorgeous, organically shaped "stones" don't have to be exact—they are perfectly imperfect by nature. While you don't need a gouge for this project, it can help you create more dips, curves, and other details in the stone. The greatest effect comes from the graining. Here, I went with a variety of woods to mimic what you'd find in a riverbed, including a beautiful buckeye burl, which has marbling that looks more like rock than wood. Mahogany and cherry round out the collection.

Carving gloves or leather thumb guard

Whittling knife

1 piece each of buckeye burl, mahogany, and cherry, cut to 3 x 3 x 3 inches

Gouge (optional)

Double-sided tape (optional)

100-, 150-, and 220-grit sandpaper, cut to 2 x 3 inches

Stain and water-resistant polyurethane coating (optional)

(continued)

1. Using the whittling knife, push-cut (see page 23) to shave off one corner of the buckeye burl by about ½ inch, cutting at a 45° angle. Repeat for all of the corners so that the wood looks like a stone **(A)**.

2. Push-cut the wood to remove each plane and facet so that it begins to look like a diamond, alternating sides to remove a little wood at a time **(B, C)**. You want to achieve an organic shape that is a little random (like that of a stone). Use the gouge to create a few shallow dips in the wood if desired.

3. Rub the wood on each sandpaper, starting with the 100 grit and ending with the 220 grit as each dulls, until the stone is flat and smooth all over **(D)**. (You can apply double-sided tape to the sandpapers and stick them to a cutting board to make this step easier.)

4. Repeat steps 1–3 for the mahogany and cherry.

5. Stain and seal the stones following the tips on page 114. (I left the buckeye burl unfinished to showcase its natural marbled grain.)

TIP: To make these into paperweight magnets, carve a hole into the bottom of each stone using a gouge, apply a little wood glue, and insert a rare-earth magnet. Place on your desk to corral paper clips.

SOAP DISH

INTERMEDIATE

ADD A LITTLE STYLE TO YOUR HOME SPA WITH A minimalist cradle for your bar of soap—or use it elsewhere as a platform for something pretty. For more stability, add cork or felt dots to the bottom. If your vanity space is tight, adjust the final size accordingly. Because this dish may see lots of moisture, I chose cypress, which is naturally water-repellent; another option is to seal pine or basswood with a water-resistant polyurethane coating (see page 115).

Pencil and ruler

1 piece of cypress wood, cut lengthwise with the grain to
2¾ x 4 x ¾ inches

Bench hook (see page 71) or F-style clamp

Carving gloves or leather thumb guard

Gouge

Whittling knife

100-, 150-, and 220-grit sandpapers, cut to 2 x 3 inches

Water-resistant polyurethane coating (optional)

(continued)

1. Using the template on page 123, draw the top, bottom, and sides of the soap dish onto the wood. Use the ruler to mark 10 dots every ¼ inch across the width of the wood. Repeat on the other short side and then connect the dots to make 10 straight lines across the width of the wood (A).

2. Position the wood on the bench hook with a short side facing you. Use the gouge to slowly cut a groove between the first two lines; try to make only one cut to get the cleanest results (B). (If you don't have a gouge, use the V cut on page 27 to get the same results.) Cut a groove between the next two lines and repeat until you have dug out 5 stripes.

3. Turn the soap dish over. Using the whittling knife, push-cut (see page 23) to whittle the wood to the pencil lines you marked on the bottom in step 1 (C). Repeat for the remaining three sides.

4. Sand the soap dish with the grain until the wood is smooth and no knife marks remain. Begin sanding with the 100 grit and work your way up to the 220 grit as each sandpaper dulls. Be sure to round each groove for an even finish (D).

5. Apply a water-resistant polyurethane coating (see page 115) to the soap dish if desired.

LIVE

CAMP

COMB

HARD

THIS HANDCRAFTED WOODEN COMB INCLUDES JUST the right details to make a beautiful gift for someone you love. The wide spacing of the teeth makes it versatile enough for a beard or long locks, and its thoughtfully placed thumb indentation ensures an easy grip. Personalize the handle by carving a monogram or an original pattern across it to make your comb unique.

Pencil

1 piece of cherry, walnut, or buckeye burl wood, cut lengthwise with the grain to 2½ x 3 x ¼ inches

Carving gloves or leather thumb guard (optional but encouraged)

Whittling knife

F-style clamp

Handsaw (see page 31)

Gouge (optional)

1 flat ⅛-inch file

1 round ⅛-inch file

100-, 150-, and 220-grit sandpapers, cut to 2 x 3 inches

Stain (optional)

(continued)

1. Using the template on page 122, draw an outline of the comb on the wood. Mark 7 lines where the teeth should go, making the middle line the longest with the outer lines increasingly shorter toward the edges. Whittle the wood with the knife to roughly the drawn shape **(A)** by using power cuts (see page 25) and push cuts (see page 23). (Another option is to use a handsaw to shape the wood.)

2. Secure the wood to the edge of your work surface with the clamp so that the penciled-in teeth are hanging off the table. Being careful not to cut the table, use the handsaw to cut along the 7 lines, creating the teeth of the comb **(B)**. You may find it easier to stand while doing this.

3. Begin whittling and refining the outline of the comb by rounding out the edges using push cuts **(C)**.

4. Put on the carving gloves. With the very thinnest part of your knife, use the push cut or the pull cut (see page 24) to carefully slice off the long edges of each tooth so that each is shaped like an octagon **(D)**.

5. If desired, use a gouge to carve out a shallow indentation where your thumb should go.

(continued)

6. Use the flat file to smooth the edges and outside of each tooth. Refine the ends of the teeth until they come to a rounded point. Insert the round file between two of the teeth, then pull the file up and over one of the teeth **(E)**. Repeat until each tooth is rounded out.

7. Sand the comb's handle and teeth with the grain until the wood is even and smooth **(F)**. Begin sanding with the 100 grit and work your way up to the 220 grit as each sandpaper dulls.

8. Personalize the comb with the stain of your choice, if desired (see page 114).

MIDCENTURY BIRD

INTERMEDIATE

I ALWAYS LOVE MAKING SIMPLE, ABSTRACT PIECES when I am traveling, and this sweet little bird is one of my favorite projects to work on around the campfire. It makes great use of any good-quality debris you find in the woods or on the beach, especially driftwood (see page 30 for tips on drying out live wood). The shape is inspired by the essential lines of the Eames House Bird, which is an icon of 1950s design—a nice update of the folksy objects with which American whittling is associated. Paint it black if you wish, or just oil it for a natural finish.

Pencil

1 piece of cedar, mahogany, or walnut wood,
cut to 3 x 3 x 3 inches

Carving gloves or a leather thumb guard

Whittling knife

100-, 150-, and 220-grit sandpapers, cut to 2 x 3 inches

Soft 100% cotton cloth

Mineral oil

(continued)

1. Using the template on page 119, draw the outline and profile of the bird onto the wood. Put on the carving gloves. Whittle the wood with the knife to roughly the drawn shape by using power cuts (see page 25) and push cuts (see page 23). (Another option is to use a handsaw to shape the wood.)

2. Carve the tail using push cuts (A). Taper its profile slightly so that it's thinner than the body.

3. Whittle the body of the bird using push cuts, giving it a round stomach and head; cut the head last (B).

4. Use push cuts to carve the beak, being especially careful as the beak will become very fragile and thin: don't cut away too much wood (C).

5. Sand the bird with the grain until the wood is even and smooth (D). Begin sanding with the 100 grit and work your way up to the 220 grit as each sandpaper dulls. Make sure to sand well where the head meets the body and the body meets the tail, so that you have smooth transitions throughout.

6. To finish, use the cotton cloth to rub the bird with a layer of mineral oil.

DICE

EASY

BRING THESE CUSTOM DICE ALONG ON YOUR NEXT camping trip (or carve them at the site) and impress everyone when the cards come out. They take only 30 minutes to make, so you can create a few sets from a bigger block of wood and gift them. I used a wood-burning pen to create the dots, but permanent marker or paint works just as well. Get creative and add numbers or symbols. Either way, it's game on!

Pencil and ruler

1 piece of ¾-inch thick walnut wood

F-style clamp

Carving gloves or leather thumb guard (optional but encouraged)

Handsaw (see page 31)

Whittling knife

Wood-burning pen (see page 112) or permanent marker

150- and 220-grit sandpapers, cut to 2 x 3 inches

Stain (optional)

(continued)

1. Using the pencil and ruler, mark the measurements for two ¾-inch squares on the wood **(A)**.

2. Clamp the wood to your work surface so it's secure, and begin cutting out each die with the handsaw **(B)**. Now you're ready to start whittling.

3. Using the whittling knife, push-cut (see page 23) the edges of each die to create a slight bevel **(C)**; beveled edges will help the dice roll more easily. If you will be using the wood-burning pen, plug it in to heat up.

4. Sand the dice with the grain until they are smooth, starting with the 150-grit and working your way up to the 220-grit as the sandpaper dulls.

5. Mark in pencil where the dots should go on each die. Practice with the wood-burning pen to evenly burn a few dots on a piece of scrap wood. Then carefully apply the tip of the wood-burning pen to each penciled dot on the dice **(D)**.

6. Personalize the dice with the stain of your choice, if desired (see page 114).

   TIP: If you choose to whittle these dice at the campsite, be sure to cut out the squares (see steps 1 and 2) before you hit the road.

CAMPING FLATWARE

HARD

FORGET PACKING THOSE PLASTIC UTENSILS AND chisel your own out of wood you bring to the campsite. All it takes is a little patience to create these two tools: the shapes are super simple, and each implement is just sharp enough to be functional. To avoid splinters, be sure to sand the pieces well before finishing and using them.

Pencil

2 pieces of cedar, walnut, or maple wood, cut lengthwise with the grain to 1 x 6½ x 1 inch (for the fork) and ¾ x 6½ x 1 inch (for the knife)

Whittling knife

F-style clamp

Handsaw (see page 31)

Gouge

Carving gloves or leather thumb guard

Smooth-cut flat file (optional)

80-, 100-, 150-, and 220-grit sandpapers, cut to 2 x 3 inches

Soft 100% cotton cloth

Food-grade mineral oil

(continued)

1. Using the templates on pages 122–123, draw the outline of the knife on the ¾ x 6½ x 1-inch piece of wood and the outline of the fork, as well as the prongs for the fork, on the 1 x 6½ x 1-inch piece of wood. Whittle the wood with the knife to roughly the drawn shapes **(A)** by using power cuts (see page 25) and push cuts (see page 23). (Another option is to use a handsaw to shape the wood.)

2. Carve the fork: Clamp the wood to your work surface with the drawn prongs hanging off the edge. Carefully saw along the drawn lines of the prongs **(B)**; use a very delicate touch because the prongs are thin.

3. Using the gouge, cut into the base of the fork's head to give it a slight scoop, until it is ⅛ inch thick **(C)**.

4. Using the whittling knife, push-cut to round out the edges and end of the handle **(D)**. Refine the transition from the handle to the head so it tapers.

5. Put on the carving gloves. Using the very tip of the knife, carefully push-cut between the prongs of the fork to separate and round them out **(E)**. Taper the end of each prong to a slight point. You can use a small flat file to get a sharper point and access the areas your knife has difficulty reaching, if desired.

(continued)

6. Carve the knife: Using the whittling knife, push-cut to rough out the handle (**F**).

7. Use push cuts to taper the end of the knife so it comes to a point (**G**). To sharpen the blade, taper it from the spine to the edge. Then run the 80-grit sandpaper along the back of the knife to give it a flat edge.

8. Sand the knife and fork with the grain until the wood is even and smooth (**H**). Begin sanding with the 100 grit and work your way up to the 220 grit as each sandpaper dulls. Be sure to sand the prongs of the fork well, so no rough edges remain.

9. Use the cotton cloth to rub the utensils with a layer of mineral oil, letting them dry for at least 30 minutes before using.

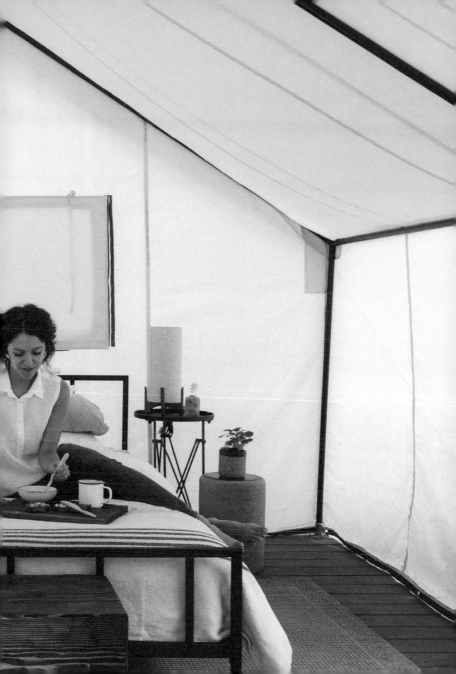

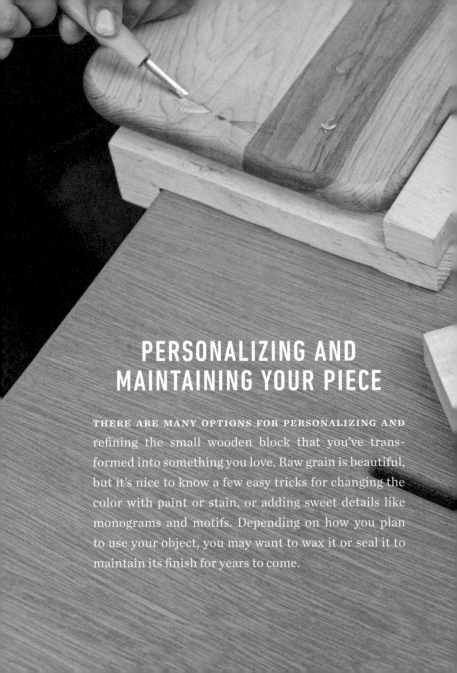

PERSONALIZING AND MAINTAINING YOUR PIECE

THERE ARE MANY OPTIONS FOR PERSONALIZING AND refining the small wooden block that you've transformed into something you love. Raw grain is beautiful, but it's nice to know a few easy tricks for changing the color with paint or stain, or adding sweet details like monograms and motifs. Depending on how you plan to use your object, you may want to wax it or seal it to maintain its finish for years to come.

BURNING WOOD

Electric wood-burning pens (like the kind used for making the dots on the dice on page 96) come in inexpensive sets with different tips for creating effects such as dots, shading, and even calligraphy. Be sure to mark your design in pencil on your project before you begin, and practice on scrap wood first. Never burn over a varnish because the finish could catch fire.

ETCHING

Use a spoon gouge to carve patterns and textures into the wood surface. Here, you see four different effects I created with just one tool: long straight lines, short straight lines, curves, and organic waves to mimic wood graining. As always, plot out the details with a pencil so you won't be sorry: draw first, cut once.

STAINING

Don't like the color of a wood? Stain it to something that suits your style. Changing the color of a wood is also a great way to elevate cheap scrap. I love to play with "stain blocking": I stain half of my object a slightly darker color than the other half (it's an idea similar to color blocking). If you have questions about a particular color you're trying to achieve, trust the experts at your local hardware store.

COATING

A water-resistant polyurethane coating is a good choice for items that will see heavy use, especially in the bathroom or the kitchen. Some brands offer one-step poly and stain coatings, so you can change the color of the wood and give it the protection that it needs at the same time (some are even available in a convenient spray can!). I recommend applying two coats for a rock-hard finish.

OILING

Once you've etched, burned, or stained the wood to your heart's content, you'll probably want to condition it to prevent it from drying out. I keep mineral oil on hand for this task. (It must be labeled "food grade" if you apply it to kitchen items used for eating.) I also like to use tung oil, Danish oil, orange oil, and linseed oil. Be aware that the oil will darken the wood slightly, but it will keep your piece from warping or cracking. Apply one coat with a 100% cotton cloth (an old T-shirt should do the trick); rub in the oil using a circular motion. Allow the item to dry, at least 30 minutes or, better, overnight. Never put your wooden item in a dishwasher or soak it in water; instead, wash the item by hand with a mild soap, dry it, and reapply the oil when necessary.

SEALING

To preserve your piece and to create a stunning finish, apply two coats of a beeswax mixture. Because wax is very difficult to clean, you'll need to dedicate a vessel for just this purpose. I use a small Crock-Pot that I found at a yard sale for five dollars, but an old pot set over a smaller pot of simmering water (to make a double boiler) will work fine.

In the pot, heat a 25/75 mixture of beeswax to mineral oil (make sure the latter is food-grade if you intend to apply it to kitchen items used for eating), stirring every 5 minutes until the wax becomes a smooth liquid. Add more oil to the beeswax mixture if you want a smoother wood butter, or add more wax if you prefer the texture of a paste.

Working with care, because the wax is hot (wear gloves if you wish), dip a 100% cotton towel or an old T-shirt in the wax and rub it in a circular motion on the wood to completely cover the object. Let the wax dry slightly, and then apply another coat. Wait about an hour to let the wax dry completely, then buff the piece with a clean 100% cotton cloth to remove any excess wax.

An object sealed with wax should be able to withstand light water exposure or food use. To revitalize it after prolonged handling, simply reapply two coats of the hot wax mixture, let it dry, and buff off excess wax. If your object sustains severe damage from water or another source, it may be necessary to sand it completely, refinish it, and reapply wax.

TEMPLATES

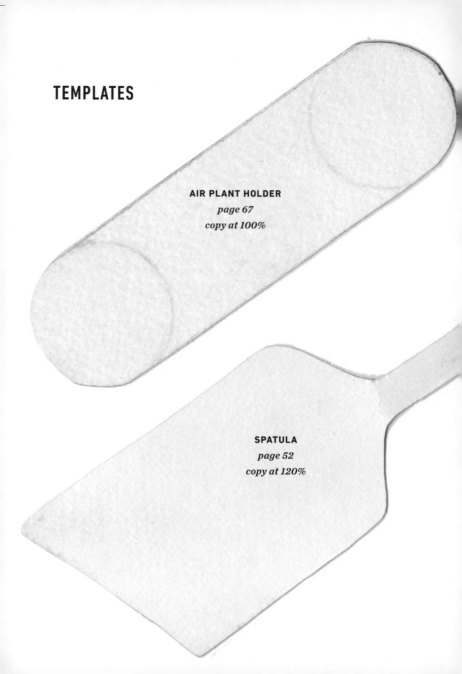

AIR PLANT HOLDER
page 67
copy at 100%

SPATULA
page 52
copy at 120%

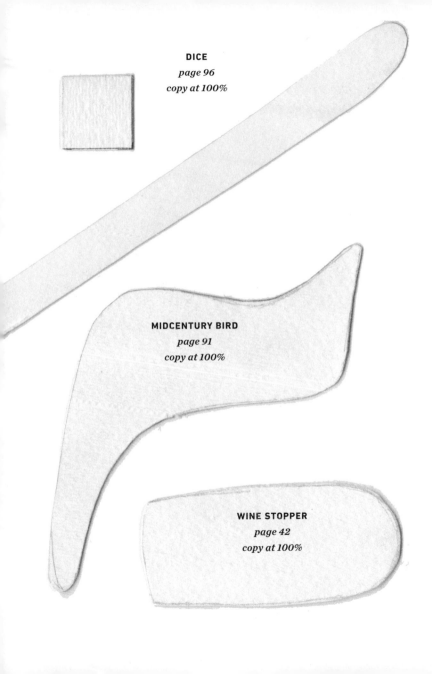

DICE
page 96
copy at 100%

MIDCENTURY BIRD
page 91
copy at 100%

WINE STOPPER
page 42
copy at 100%

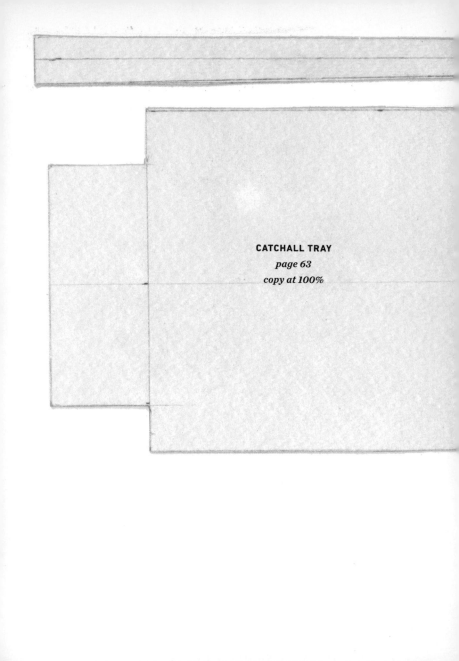

CATCHALL TRAY
page 63
copy at 100%

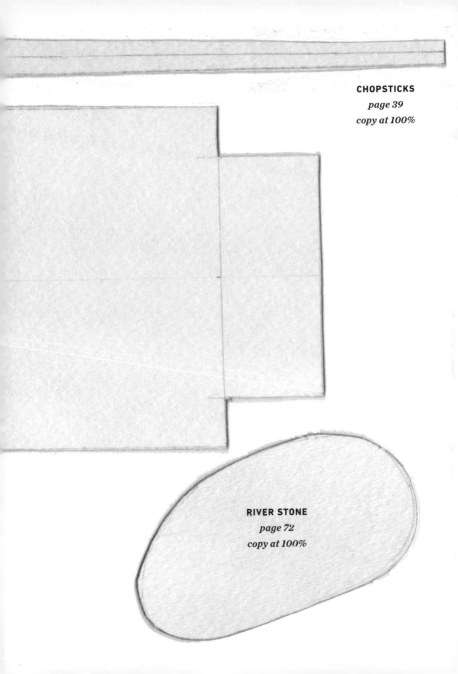

CHOPSTICKS
page 39
copy at 100%

RIVER STONE
page 72
copy at 100%

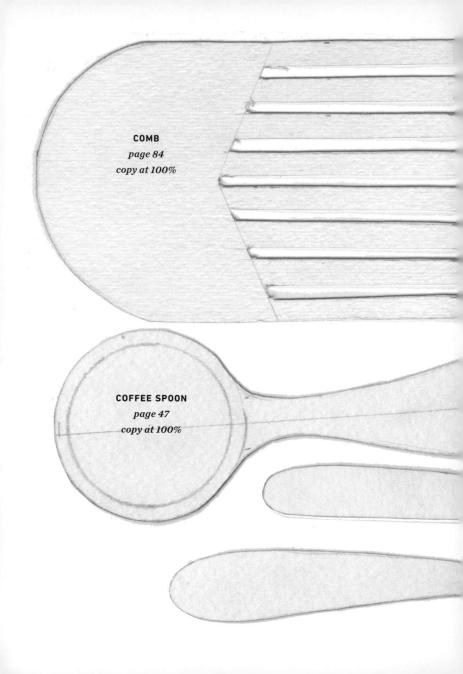

COMB
page 84
copy at 100%

COFFEE SPOON
page 47
copy at 100%

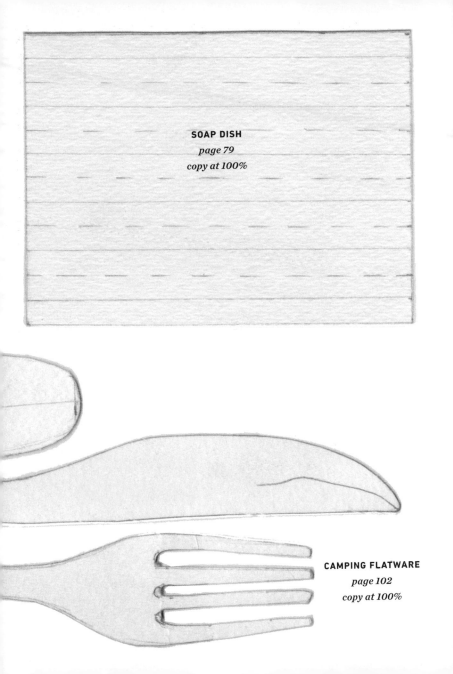

SOAP DISH
page 79
copy at 100%

CAMPING FLATWARE
page 102
copy at 100%

SOURCEBOOK

Melanie Abrantes Designs
www.melanieabrantes.com
You can find everything you
need to whittle on my website,
from my Japanese cutting tools
to spoon kits.

Amazon
www.amazon.com
A great source for wood, whittling tools, stains—you name
it—with bargain pricing to boot.

Craigslist
www.craigslist.org
If you're on a budget, check
out the garage-sale section for
secondhand tools.

EstateSale.com
www.estatesale.com
I've found many well-cared-for
tools through this site; keep an
eye out for any local sales.

Garrett Wade
www.garrettwade.com
A quality source for woodworking tools and project supplies.

Hida Tool & Hardware Co.
www.hidatool.com
This fantastic woodworking
shop in Berkeley, California, is
my source for Japanese tools.

Highland Woodworking
www.highlandwoodworking.com
I purchase carving tools and
supplies from this Atlanta-
based woodworking specialist.

The Home Depot
www.homedepot.com
This big-box retailer has a
decent wood and tool selection
both online and in stores.

Japan Woodworker
www.japanwoodworker.com
This importer of Japanese
wood-carving tools offers a
great selection for hobbyists
and professionals alike.

**Jo-Ann Fabric and
Craft Stores**
www.joann.com
Check out the website for inexpensive wood pieces and starter
tool kits.

**Little Shavers Wood Carving
Supply**
www.littleshavers.com
This mail-order wood-carving
supply company stocks everything you need for whittling.

Lowe's
www.lowes.com
You'll find a decent selection of wood and tools both online and in stores.

MacBeath Hardwood
www.macbeath.com
I purchase my wood at this lumberyard, which has stores in California, Indiana, and Salt Lake City. (Check out their amazing scrap bins!)

Michaels Stores
www.michaels.com
This chain stocks plenty of pine and basswood cuts for spoons and other small projects.

Rockler Woodworking and Hardware
www.rockler.com
Everything you need to whittle—from lumber to woodworking books to tools—is available at this specialty source, along with very knowledgeable employees to help you get started.

Woodcraft Supply
www.woodcraft.com
Check out this supplier's extensive online catalog of woodworking tools and lumber.

Woodworker's Supply
www.woodworker.com
Whether your project is simple or complex, this source will help you find the right tool.

OTHER RESOURCES

The following books have inspired me to learn more about whittling and wood carving:

Beiderman, Charles, and William Johnston. *The Beginner's Handbook of Woodcarving.* New York: Dover, 1988.

Luhkemann, Chris. *The Little Book of Whittling.* East Petersburg, PA: Fox Chapel Publishing, 2013.

Odate, Toshio. *Japanese Woodworking Tools.* Fresno: Linden, 1998.

Tangerman, F. J. *Whittling and Woodcarving.* New York: McGraw-Hill, 1936.

Tesolin, Vic. *The Minimalist Woodworker.* Nashville: Spring House Press, 2015.

Tomashek, Steve. *Tiny Whittling.* Chicago: Chicago Review Press, 2012.

ACKNOWLEDGMENTS

Mom, Dad, Chris, and Melissa, thank you for your endless support of my creative endeavors. You have listened to me talk about all of my projects, even without understanding exactly what they are. I love you! Dan and Adrian, you are the two best friends a girl could ask for. Thank you for always encouraging me and listening during my moments of self-doubt. Farrah, Kylie, and Denisse, thank you for being my lifelong cheerleaders. I love you like sisters.

To Silvia Song: You always seem to know how to solve a problem, and you've taken care of me as if I were your little sister. You are such a talented designer, and I am always in awe of your brilliant, creative mind. To Emma Brooks: You've always inspired me to work hard and hustle! Thank you for helping me understand the book world and agreeing to be a model in my photographs.

To Genevieve: I am so happy to have you by my side. Thank you for being my right hand, friend, and colleague. You helped make this book as beautiful as it could be—putting more than you had to into every image and project and even graciously letting us shoot in your home. Thank you for believing in me and encouraging me as I worked on this book (I know I can be whiny!). To Melanie Riccardi: Thank you for being such a positive and calm presence in my life. I love that we have developed such an amazing relationship as friends and collaborators. Your photography perfectly captured my work and made it even better. Thank you from the bottom of my heart for your friendship and love. I also want to thank Jenny Morgan, for helping with the photo shoots: Your talent and personality make you a joy to work with.

To my editor, Angelin Borsics: Thank you for your help and guidance throughout the publishing process. Your expertise, patience, and involvement in every aspect of this book made it happen. I am also grateful to designer Stephanie Huntwork, production manager Kim Tyner, and production editorial director Mark McCauslin at Clarkson Potter, for making this book come together in a beautiful and timely manner.

To Ryan Miller at AutoCamp: Thank you for your generosity—you let us use your space in Russian River, and worked with us to make it happen on short notice. You even stepped in when we needed another male model! California is lucky to have such a cool camping experience.

To Mukesh Prasad: Thank you for always mentoring me and supporting my crazy wood-turning ideas. You're the best adopted grandfather a girl could ask for! To Tanya Aguiniga: Thank you for being such a strong, independent woman in my life. Without your courageousness, I wouldn't have seen that it's possible to be a successful maker and business owner.

A big thanks to everyone at MacBeath Hardwood for their friendly faces and for the generous discount on the wood used to make the projects in this book.

I am grateful to the product design department at Otis College of Art and Design for fostering my creativity and letting me be who I wanted to be even before I knew what that was for myself. And to *Sweet Paul* and The Makerie: Thank you for believing in me and my woodworking class; without you, Angelin might never have found me!

Last but not least, thank you to friendly strangers and fans of my work, for supporting me and tagging along on this crazy adventure. You guys are the best!

ACKNOWLEDGMENTS

Whittle a beautiful spoon, comb, pair of dice, and other small iconic objects with this fresh introduction to a folksy craft. Along the way, you'll learn how to choose the right knife and grain of wood; you'll also attain helpful information on safety and techniques for refining your piece. Whether you're headed to the woods or just to the porch, this pocket-size guide will have you carving your own unique designs in no time.

MELANIE ABRANTES teaches wood carving at workshops in Oakland, California. She sells her designs in small shops and retail stores nationwide, and her work has been featured in *Domino, Dwell, Bon Appétit*, and more. Visit her at melanieabrantes.com.